My Fellow Americans . . .

My Fellow Americans . . .

by Jeff Jacobson

Afterword by Russell Lockhart

University of New Mexico Press
in association with
PICTURE PROJECT, Inc.

Picture Project gratefully acknowledges generous support from Harold Eisenman, *Fortune Magazine* in memory of Ethan Hoffman, National Endowment for the Arts, and New York State Council on the Arts.

Edited and designed by Picture Project, Inc.
40 West 12th Street
New York, New York 10011.
Editors: Abigail Heyman and Ethan Hoffman
Editorial Assistant: Meryl Levin
Designer: Lorraine Ferguson

Produced and distributed by University of New Mexico Press
1720 Lomas Boulevard, NE
Albuquerque, New Mexico 87131.
Printed in Japan by Dai Nippon.

A traveling exhibiton of *My Fellow Americans* . . . has been organized by Musée de l'Elysée, Lausanne, Switzerland.

Library of Congress Cataloging in Publication Data
Jacobson, Jeff, 1946–
My fellow Americans.
Jeff Jacobson: Afterword by Russell Lockhart, p. 109
ISBN 0–8263–1292–6 (cloth)
ISBN 0–8263–1293–4 (paper)
1. United States—Description and travel—1981—Views.
2. Jacobson, Jeff, 1946–,
—Journeys—United States.
I. Title.
E169.04.J34 1991 91–9521
917.304' 928—dc20 CIP

(cover)
Grandfather and Grandson
Naples, Florida 1981

(frontispiece)
Alan and Dixie Hatfield
Matewan, West Virginia 1978

I dedicate this book to Ethan,
who in death taught me about the preciousness of life,
and to Marnie and Henry,
who are as precious to me as life itself.

J.J.

Crow Fair
Crow Indian Reservation
Montana 1987

Introduction

America rests upon the myth of the American Dream—that it is the God-given right of every one of us to have a slice of the ever expanding American Pie. Our politicians, preachers, and educators support this myth by assuring us that we Americans are a grand, good, and just people. They always locate the focus of evil outside of us: Russians, Saddam Hussein, terrorists, secular humanists. "This is THE GREATEST COUNTRY on the face of the earth!" and "Jesus is the ONLY way!" Evil and the devil are projected onto the world, while decency and God reign at home. This myth worked fairly well so long as there were enough Indians to kill, prairies to pave, communists to arm against, and women to protect. As of late, it appears a bit dated.

Sometimes societies hold onto their myths too long. A myth loses its power as the reality changes. In the same way, individuals have myths that outlast their usefulness.

I simultaneously feel deeply at home in this country and like a perpetual visitor to a strange and bizarre land. The twin specters of Hitler and the atom bomb cast shadows over my childhood. I was born in Iowa, in 1946, the second son of first-generation American Jewish parents who were trying to assimilate into a predominantly Christian culture. As a young boy I was usually the only Jewish kid in my class at school. Anti-Semitism occasionally rose to the surface. My few Jewish friends developed a sense of black humor to deal with the legacy of the Nazis, calling each other "bars of soap" or "lampshades." I devoured biographies of Indian leaders: Crazy Horse, Sitting Bull, Red Cloud, Cochise, Geronimo, Chief Joseph. I discovered an American tradition of genocide. I felt a connection to American society, but along with it came a sense of menace.

My parents grew up with confused myths: they fled the Old Country ways of their own mothers and fathers yet did not quite fit into the shiny new model of the American Dream. Their generation had it hard. The Depression, Hitler, and Freud frightened them, while powerful immigrant parents were breathing down their necks.

As a child, my role within my family was that of The OK Kid. I was quiet, undemanding; I was assumed to have very few problems. I learned to blend into the woodwork. (This survival tactic would later serve me well as a photographer.) I hid out from parents, teachers, relatives, and, most unfortunately, girls. More importantly, I was also completely hidden from myself. The myth of The OK Kid began to unravel during a boozy adolescence, highlighted by occasional brushes with the law. Fears of dealing with women, and of being alone, led to a failed first marriage. In 1973, I was an American Civil Liberties Union lawyer in Atlanta. My heart was in it politically and intellectually, but I couldn't bear the slow, methodical, confining nature of legal practice. My life lacked passion. I needed a hobby. I bought a camera.

As the conflict between the cultural myth of the American Dream and the reality of American life became too great to ignore, so did the gulf between my personal myth as The OK Kid and the truth of my everyday life. And when a myth no longer supports the reality, it's time to junk the myth. So making photographs became a process of myth debunking, both individual and cultural.

I began photographing in rural Georgia jails while working for the ACLU. Danny Lyon's pictures of the Texas prison system, in his book *Conversations with the Dead*, hit me like a bolt from the blue. I spent more and more time making photographs and less and less time with the law. The final blow to my legal career came when I journeyed to Millerton, New York, for a workshop with Charles Harbutt. Among other lessons, Charlie showed me that photographers could take good pictures and still earn a living. What a revelation! My passion could be my career.

Two years later, in 1976, I was at a George Wallace rally in Boston. I was just beginning to shoot color film, and color made me nervous. I needed to loosen up and enjoy it. So I played! I let the shutter run, jiggled the camera, waved the thing all over the place. Another revelation! The traditional forms of photography weren't binding rules.

I followed the presidential primaries throughout the country. While shooting Jimmy Carter in a Cuban joint in Miami, I added strobe to the mix. The strobe heightened the sense of time in my photographs. Combined with a long shutter speed, the strobe allowed me to glimpse not only the moment the subject was illuminated by the flash, but also the moments immediately before and after. This technique created a sense of time moving within a single frame. It also gave the photographs a three-dimensional look by making the foreground jump away from the background. For a while this technique alone fascinated me, but I soon learned that the technique is only useful to the extent that the picture beneath it has meaning.

I continued photographing in the United States, refining my technique. I sought out public events where the emotions underlying American mythology become visible. I shot political conventions and presidential inaugurations, the Miss America Pageant, baby parades, college football games, blues festivals, charity balls. I photographed the preachers and priests who filled their cash registers by proclaiming the glory of god and country. I rattled around in the dark underbelly of the American psyche with the Christian Patriots Defense League:

Louisville, Illinois, July 1984

I'm with about a thousand people under a tent on a sweltering summer night. They are listening in rapture as the leader of the Christian Patriots Defense League rants his hatred of "Satan's Children," the Jews. I am the only photographer shooting, standing in a no man's land between the crowd and the speaker. His eyes narrow, his focus falls upon me, and, spitting his venom against Jews, says, "I can sense when they're around me. My skin crawls." I do the only thing left to me. I press the shutter and nail him right between the eyes with the flash from my strobe. It is Friday night. I do not wish him good Shabbas.

The next day, a Defense League general, looking at my press tag, asks me suspiciously, "Jacobson, Jacobson. That's a Swedish name, isn't it?" I look at him, smile, and in perfect conscience reply, "Yes it is." What I don't tell him is that my grandfather, on a stopover in Sweden on his way to America from his native Poland, ditched his family name, Shillabolsky, and adopted Jacobson. A man with great foresight, my grandfather.

Later that day I'm with a Christian Patriot and his two bored children on maneuvers in the forest. He is scanning the bushes with his binoculars, searching for any Jews who might be lurking nearby. Little does he realize, there is one in the next bush over, armed with a camera.

One group chosen to play the role of sacrificial lamb in the eighties was small, family farmers. They had been the original embodiment of the American myth. Throughout the postwar period, an unholy alliance of government and agribusiness urged American farmers to increase production, buy new equipment, and dump huge amounts of expensive chemical fertilizers, pesticides, and herbicides on their land. Most American farmers bought this program. In the early eighties, land values and commodity prices plummeted, and many heavily mortgaged farmers lost their farms. The same government that had led them down this primrose path now wouldn't lift a finger to help them:

Algona, Iowa, January 1985
This auction is the most heartbreaking yet. They fit the profile—a young farm couple who had to take out heavy loans to get started and couldn't meet the payments when prices and land values fell. These people are the latest casualties in a relentless series of foreclosures sweeping small, family farmers off their land.

After the auction I talk to a neighbor, a man in his sixties. He complains bitterly about the government's failure to help the small farmer. I ask him who he'd voted for in the recent election.

"Reagan," he answers.

"Why?" I ask.

"Abortion," he replies.

I am absolutely dumbfounded. He and all his neighbors are being driven off their land, and he wants to use what little power he has, his voting power, to control women.

Abortion is an emotionally difficult issue, but I think it's a convenient cover for a deeper agenda: the perpetuation of patriarchy and male supremacy. I left that farm auction convinced that the problem of male supremacy is a thread that links most of the major issues facing America today. The American Dream was primarily intended as a myth for men. It was men, after all, who were expected to do the lion's share of Indian killing, prairie paving, and redbaiting.

The American Dream is but the latest historical variation of this male myth. Remember, it was Eve who ate the apple from the tree of knowledge of good and evil, thereby forcing our male God to boot basically blameless Adam, with his offending female, out of the Garden of Eden. God further ordered us men to assume dominion and control over these obviously irresponsible women, and to begin begetting like crazy. Very few men questioned this arrangement over the next five thousand or so years. Lately, however, many women, and some men, have begun to wonder about its wisdom. Some of my own questions find their way into my pictures.

If conditions were deteriorating for the family farmer in the Midwest, they had long ago hit bottom for the migrant farmworkers who travel the harvest circuit. I spent some time in Belle Glade and Immokalee, two Florida towns far more similar to Haiti or Mexico than to the rest of the United States:

Immokalee, Florida, January 1981
A severe freeze has destroyed most of the winter vegetable crop, so that there is very little work for the already desperately poor migrant workers who have come to this dusty southwest Florida town. I do not have an assignment; I am doing some shooting here on my own. A man I meet at a farmworkers union office offers to take me to a particularly nasty migrant camp. We walk in on a scene of pure beauty amidst the squalor: two young girls, bathed in soft evening

light, are braiding the hair of their elderly grandmother. Before I can take a picture, my guide tells them that I am a journalist who has come to expose their living conditions. Bedlam ensues. You'd think I am the Second Coming. I frantically try to explain that I'm no savior; in fact, I don't even have a proper journalistic assignment. At the same time, I desperately try to make a picture before the rapidly fading light disappears. I make two frames. Then they take me to their shack to show me their food supply—one dead pigeon, which they had killed the day before, lies forlornly in their tiny refrigerator. I feel awful and try to explain that there is very little likelihood that my photographs will have any impact on their lives. But just the fact that a white man with cameras has come to their camp seems miraculous to them.

This incident has taught me a lesson. Whenever I see photographers proudly claiming the mantle of the "concerned photographer," warning flags go up for me. I've learned that no matter how good or noble the intentions of the photographer are in righting some social wrong, the interest being served first and foremost is the photographer's, not the subject's. That's not to say that sometimes people can't be helped by the publication of photographs. The powerful images of starvation in Ethiopia, for example, probably helped save thousands of lives. I don't argue against photographers being motivated by feelings of compassion and a desire to confront the issues of the day. In fact, I am usually motivated by just such feelings myself. But these feelings, when unchecked, can lead photographers to grandiosity, exploitation of the subject, and boring pictures.

By the early 1980s, I had remarried and become a father. As our marriage deepened, and our son grew, I continually photographed my family:

Naples, Florida, June 1983

I see my father wildly throwing Henry up and down in the smooth Gulf of Mexico water. I charge in and make a few quick frames. On the way out I notice that my strobe is on the wrong setting. I know that moment was special, and I can't recreate it.

Later, back home and editing the film with a friend, I see that the flash has slightly overexposed Henry and my father and say that it's too bad, because it could have been such a nice photograph. "Schmuck!" my friend shouts. "That makes the picture!" I realized that the accident has lifted my father and son out of the facts of the situation and given them an angelic quality that makes them far more profound and symbolic.

This photograph helped heal a long-standing breach between my father and me. Though close to me in my childhood, my father had grown disenchanted with me since my teenage years—or, as he put it, "since puberty reared its ugly head." But my son became the joy of his life, and when I gave him a print of this photograph, he began to understand the power I feel with the camera.

I do feel power in the camera, power in photographs. I'm not always aware of where that power originates, but I don't leave my unconscious at home when I photograph. I pack it in my suitcase, along with the toothbrush, film, and 28mm lens. When my pictures really work, they reveal information about myself as well as the world. My best pictures occur when I find an unconscious truth of my own that connects with, the reality I see in the world. These pictures do not come from careful calculation; they are immediate responses to the world. The best pictures I feel; they come from the heart and the gut as well as the head.

Photography has a certain relation to time and to the world that is unique among the arts. A photograph can describe the world at a specific moment in time, yet contain a powerful ambiguity. This ambiguity comes from the meeting of the photographer's psyche with the world's reality. Whose truth is being presented in the photograph —that of the photographer or that of the world? This tension empowers viewers to interpret the photograph's reality for themselves.

My photographs are not reality. They are a record of how I interpreted reality and how I formally arranged that interpretation in the frame at the moment of exposure. My best pictures result from the wedding of my unconscious to my camera: they are as close to dreams as they are to journalism.

Journalism tries to contain and direct the meaning of photographs with captions, context, lack of individual style, and literal storytelling. Photographs are too often mistaken for words or facts by the text editors who control their usage. They are used to illustrate text. They become redundant.

We also tend to associate color in photographs with facts, because of the predominance of color in journalism and advertising, both of which pretend to transmit facts. As a color photographer, my challenge is not to get stuck in the facts presented in the pictures. I want my pictures to give me information about the world while allowing me to transcend that information and play in the realm of my imagination. This requires an abstraction. In black and white this abstraction is immediate, because the world exists in color. Color photographs require a different kind of abstraction. My challenge is to accentuate color without letting it so dominate my pictures that the subject matter of my photography becomes color itself. It's a delicate balancing act.

For me, life itself is a delicate balancing act. I am constantly balancing my needs to be with my family, to see my friends, to make money, and to photograph as I choose. Photography is the fulcrum of my balancing act. It keeps me sane. Photography can be hard, lonely work, and it is also a great joy. The world just seems right to me when I have a camera in my hand.

There are photographs in this book that make me smile, and painful pictures that I don't like to look at too long, or too closely. Yet making and looking at these pictures is one way I can know my own psyche, and the collective psyche of America. Maybe by getting to know those painful parts, we can stop projecting them out onto the world, where they have a tendency to rebound back at us, hard and fast. Maybe we can change our myths about ourselves.

America's myths, I hope, are in a state of transformation. As old myths die, new ones tend to arise with a force of their own to meet the changed conditions. In thinking about a new myth for America, and for myself, I think of the poem "Power and Love," by Martin Buber:

1
Our hope is too new and too old—
I do not know what would remain to us
Were love not transfigured power
And power not straying love.

2
Do not protest: "Let love alone rule!"
Can you prove it true?
But resolve: Every morning
I shall concern myself anew about the boundary
Between the love-deed-Yes and the power-deed-No
And pressing forward honor reality.

3
We cannot avoid
Using power,
Cannot escape the compulsion
To afflict the world,
So let us, cautious in diction
and mighty in contradiction
Love powerfully.

Making the photographs in this book has been a process of confronting some of my own personal demons, and some collective American ones, and feeling all of their grips on me loosening. It's like an exorcism, except I'm not trying to cast the devils out; I'm trying to know and own the devils within. And let the devils lead me to the angels.

Jeff Jacobson

National Conservative Political
Action Committee Dinner
Inauguration of President Reagan
Washington, D.C. 1985

And I dreamed I was dying
And I dreamed that my soul rose unexpectedly
And looking back down at me
Smiled reassuringly
And I dreamed I was flying
And high above my eyes could clearly see
The Statue of Liberty
Sailing away to sea
And I dreamed I was flying

Paul Simon
American Tune

St. George, Utah 1981

MOTEL
El Peso
FAMILY UNITS

(left)
Iowa Girls High School Basketball
Tournament
Des Moines, Iowa 1979

(right)
Watertown, Massachusetts 1983

LAND OF
LIBERTY

Ralston-Purina Company
St. Louis, Missouri 1985

Cat Gymnasium
Carnation Company
Seattle, Washington 1985

Saturday Night Beach Party
La Jolla, California 1985

Catholic Charismatic Healing
Service
Cleveland, Ohio 1987

Texas vs. Oklahoma
Dallas, Texas 1983

SOONERS
75

Mississippi Delta Blues Festival
Greenville, Mississippi 1983

Cajun Dance Hall
Basile, Louisiana 1984

Miss America Pageant
Atlantic City, New Jersey 1983

Atlantic City, New Jersey 1983

(left)
Miss Rattlesnake Charmer
Sweetwater Rattlesnake Roundup
Sweetwater, Texas 1984

(opposite)
Halloween Party
New York City 1982

The Baby Parade
Ocean City, New Jersey 1983

Cabbage Patch Birthing Center
New York City 1985

Chicken
OF THE
Sea
BRAND
RECIPE ON BACK

(left)
Enterprise Square
Oklahoma City, Oklahoma 1984

(right)
Taste Testers
Carnation Company
Seattle, Washington 1985

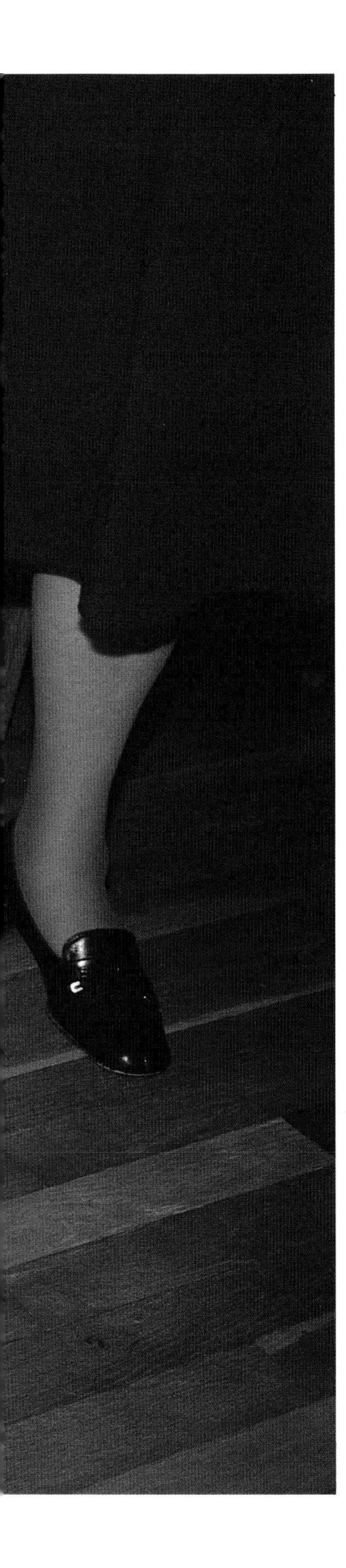

(left)
Thanksgiving Dinner
Weathersfield Bow, Vermont 1979

(right)
Fashion Show
Museum of Natural History
New York City 1981

Democratic National Convention
New York City 1976

Florida vs. LSU
Baton Rouge, Louisiana 1985

Church Service
Hilo, Hawaii 1988

Gathering of American Jewish
Holocaust Survivors
Washington, D.C. 1985

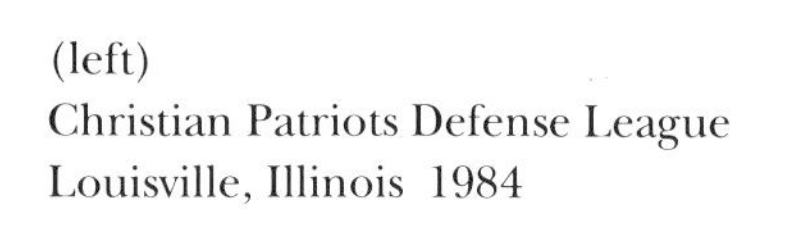

(left)
Christian Patriots Defense League
Louisville, Illinois 1984

(right)
Bathroom, Cocktail Party
Republican National Convention
Dallas, Texas 1984

Pine Ridge Sioux Reservation
Porcupine, South Dakota 1989

Reception, Daughters of the
American Revolution
Inauguration of President Reagan
Washington, D.C. 1985

Democratic National Convention
New York City 1980

Church Service
Baltimore, Maryland 1985

(left)
Cajun Mardi Gras
Mamou, Louisiana 1984

(opposite)
Inaugural Parade
Inauguration of President Reagan
Washington, D.C. 1981

ONE WAY
DIVISION
3,5
BUS PARKING
ON LEFT SIDE
OF STREET
ONLY

Bathroom, Inaugural Ball
Inauguration of President Reagan
Washington, D.C. 1985

Saturday Night
Pritikin Diet Center
Miami Beach, Florida 1984

Iowa State Fair
Des Moines, Iowa 1978

Republican National Convention
Dallas, Texas 1984

A Republican Party
Neiman-Marcus Department Store
Republican National Convention
Dallas, Texas 1984

United States Naval Academy
Annapolis, Maryland 1986

Cuban Masked Ball
Miami, Florida 1980

Cattlemen's East Ball
Palm Beach, Florida 1984

(left)
Anti-Death Penalty Vigil
Execution of Velma Barfield
North Carolina Central Prison
Raleigh, North Carolina 1984

(opposite)
South Bronx Peoples Convention
New York City, 1980

Dedication of the Vietnam
War Memorial
Washington, D.C. 1982

(left)
American Indian Vietnam
Veterans Convention
Shawnee, Oklahoma 1989

(opposite)
Congressional Medal of Honor
(Posthumous)
Chesterfield, Massachusetts 1982

Longines

Shopping Mall
Reagan Campaign Rally
Los Angeles, California 1976

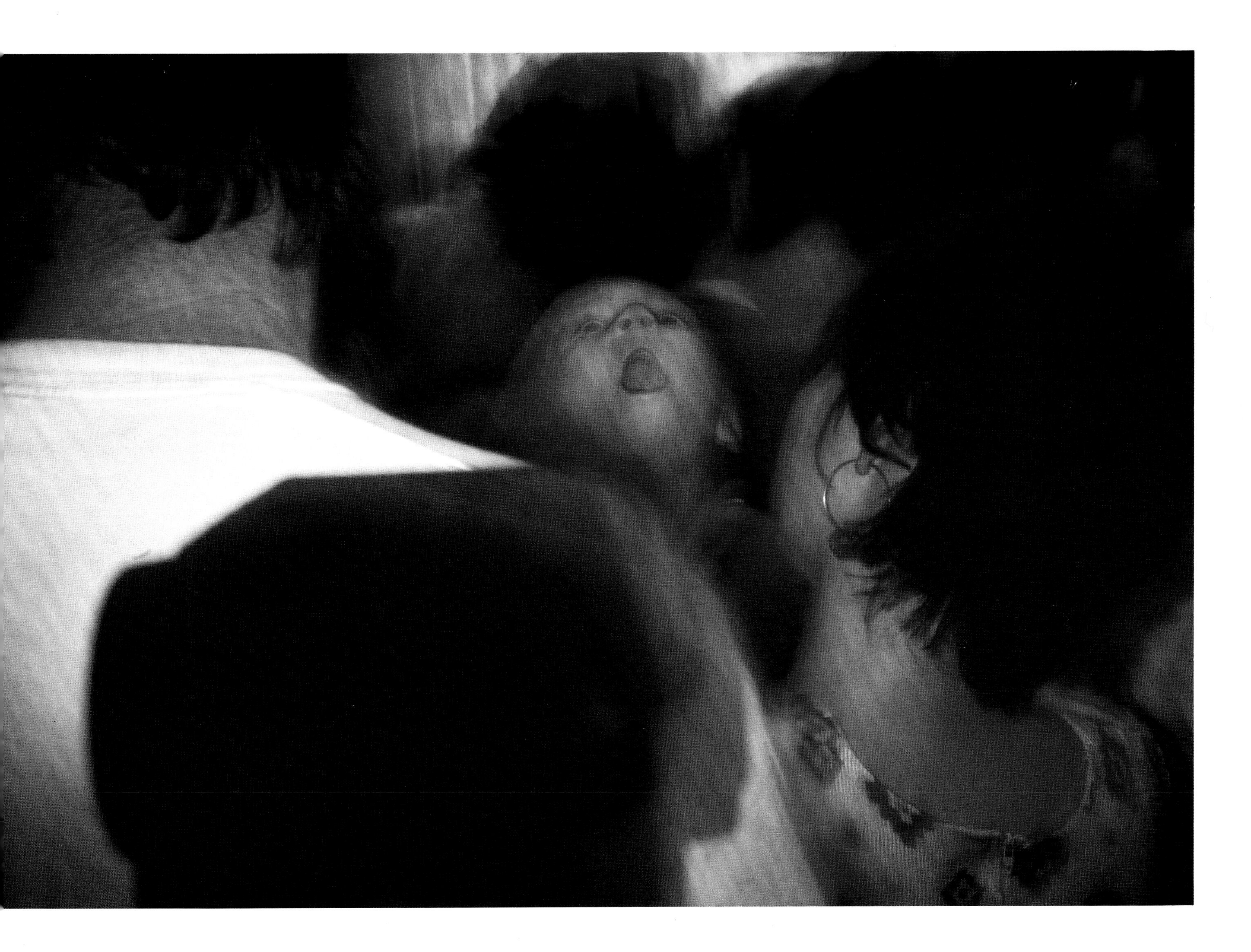

(left)
Senator Strom Thurmond
Republican National Convention
Dallas, Texas 1984

(opposite)
Deer Farm
Depauville, New York 1985

Cajun Mardi Gras
Mamou, Louisiana 1984

Longhorn Cattle Auction
Grand Ballroom
Westin Galleria Hotel
Houston, Texas 1983

62

Catholic Charismatic Healing
Service
Worcester, Massachusetts 1987

Farm Foreclosure Auction
Flandreau, South Dakota 1985

Foreclosed Farmer
Battle Creek, Iowa 1983

Hermosa, South Dakota 1989

Farm Foreclosure Auction
Algona, Iowa 1985

Strike
International Paper Company
Jay, Maine 1988

Migrant Farmworker Camp
Immokalee, Florida 1983

Refrigerator
Migrant Farmworker Camp
Immokalee, Florida 1983

32nd Precinct, Harlem
New York City 1989

Kitchen
Washington Hilton Hotel
Washington, D.C. 1989

Birth Defect
Downwind from American
Nuclear Test Site
St. George, Utah 1981

Pittsfield Egg Festival
Pittsfield, Maine 1981

ITTSFIEL

Bath Time
New York City 1981

Dairy Farm
Weathersfield Bow, Vermont 1980

Naples, Florida 1983

Grandfather and Grandson
Naples, Florida 1981

Afterword

. . . a sense of menace.

My wished end is, by gentle concussion,
the emulsion of truth.
J. Robinson, 1658

I looked at Michelangelo's *David* standing serenely in the yellow light of the rotunda of the Accademia in Florence, and, like many of those around him, took his picture. It was almost a helpless gesture, a kind of *defeat* in the face of perfection. The more I took his picture, the more I understood Susan Sontag's accusation that the photographer *appropriates* reality, making it one's own, without permission. By some odd reversal, I became tiny David conquering this Goliath of immaculate perfection. Capturing him from every angle, I was making him my own; yet I felt my obsessive gestures were also covering over a deepening anxiety about something *not done*. After all, Michelangelo created this statue, brought forth his image *into the world*, in stone. I was reduced to taking a picture, making an image of an image, an uneasy dependency on his creation. The more I clicked, the more I felt something *in*appropriate in what I was doing. I recognized too the rising envy underlying all Philistine neglect of art and culture. What I was not feeling was love.

It was in this mixture of victory and defeat that I finally saw Michelangelo's incomplete stone sculptures lining the halls of the Accademia. I was transfixed to the point of forgetting, forgetting to capture them with my camera. I took those statues home with me only in memory, remembering now my tearing eyes when I saw those rough figures struggling for existence, trying to escape their stone prison. Ignoring the crowd, I sat next to one of the sculptures and touched it, realizing with a shudder what I had not with my shutter, that I was touching something Michelangelo had touched but not finished, had *not* brought to perfection. I guess the crowd did hold me back from what I felt like doing. I wanted to kiss that figure. I was feeling love.

At home, I took the best color slide of *David*, put it in my enlarger, and created a large black and white print. I named this image *Black David*, maybe to spite my second-grade teacher for punishing my liking black best! This photograph has captivated me for years, particularly the radiating auras of light I didn't see when I was there. I've loved this image in ways I never loved Michelangelo's masterpiece. But this furtive inversion proved costly, for after making this *Black David*, my intense involvement in photography—born in childhood with making box cameras, taking pictures of insects, making telescopes, taking pictures of the heavens, and publishing all these with commentary and explanation in a mimeographed magazine sold to parents and neighbors—all this enthusiasm *died*.

It was a bit of lore from my childhood that my great, great grandfather, Nathaniel Howard Talbot, was not only a commanding officer in the Union Army during the Civil War, but also a photographer and related to, as my mother told me, "the man who invented the camera." The former story proved true enough, as I won a four-year college scholarship from the Ladies Auxiliary of the Grand Army of the Republic. I've never questioned the second tale, this possible relation to "the man who invented the camera." Oh, I know that William Henry Fox Talbot did not invent the camera. I also know that I've repeated to others, as I do now, this mythology from my childhood without the least bit of evidence for its truth

—except for those mysterious photographs in my possession of the Indian tribes of New Mexico so obviously taken more than a century ago. The truth is, I've not wanted to lose this piece of my childhood. I've had the fantasy that, cocoonlike, it carries my future connection to photography. So I've left it unexplored, accepting Freud's dictum that what a child *believes* is more crucial than raw facts; it is this *personal* mythology that becomes the chief architect of one's interior reality and one's relation to and desire for the world.

I could have become a photographer. Instead, I became a psychologist and then a psychoanalyst in the Jungian tradition. The startling invitation to write an essay for Jeff Jacobson's *My Fellow Americans . . .*, and the unsettling experiences with his excruciating photographs, reawakened my desire for photography and for my great, great grandfather. And while Jacobson's photographs have returned my passion for the photographic arts to me, I realize with a certain sadness that I am no photographer and never will be. As I look at *My Fellow Americans . . .*, that paralyzing *viewer's* envy I felt at *David*'s feet eats at me again.

Still, whatever muse informs this most democratic of arts has put the camera in my hand again and, with no more skill than enthusiasm, allows me to capture the world. When I first saw Kodak's new disposable camera, I raged at this display of consumer waste, vowing never to buy one. But as I looked and looked at Jacobson's photographs, my eye hunger increased and began devouring such things as photo books and magazines. My eye grabbed a piece by Alfred Blaker in which he told of keeping these disposables and learning to *reuse* them. So, vow broken, I bought one —a Kodak "Stretch"—and rushed home to my pond to take a bunch of pictures, just so I could reuse this disposable, to revel in revenge. As I framed the first image of the rock wall I had built on the lip of my pond, about to trip the shutter, into the viewfinder came a heron, landing in the center of my picture! The shutter clicked with the heron's wings spread wide, stretched just like my film. I was astonished at this image, stunned at this amazing intrusion on my intention. My reawakened fascination had become animated indeed! Spontaneously, I imagined the heron *wanted* to be in my photograph. That's crazy. But I couldn't deny a rising tide of feeling in response to this curious event that here was not just a "lucky accident," and certainly not my waiting for the "decisive moment," but something of the world responding *autonomously*, confirming in some strange, mysteriously synchronous way my reawakened photographic desire so obviously engendered by *My Fellow Americans . . . .* I hurriedly finished the roll and rushed down to the instant photo place so I could have my pictures in an hour. "Speed and instant aren't so bad after all," I said to myself. Later, I was told that the stretch film had to be sent to a special place for processing and it would be three to four *weeks* before I would have my pictures. No speed, no instant after all. Crestfallen and deflated, enthusiasm waning, I sensed gradually that in this series of events, if I could plumb them sufficiently, I might find the key to what *wanted* to be said in writing about *My Fellow Americans . . . .*

But why should a psychologist be asked to write about a photographer's art? There is a well-entrenched tradition for other photographers to take on this responsibility or for writers and poets to do so. Recall Jack Kerouac's introduction to Robert Frank's *The Americans*, or Carl Sandburg's introduction to *The Family of Man*, or James Agee's more elaborate work in Walker Evans' *Let Us Now Praise Famous Men*. As far as I can tell, there is no precedent for a psychologist to carry out this task. Why all these words from an analyst after looking at photographs? This unfamiliar responsibility has troubled me deeply. Am I to write through my professional lens and report on what is seen through the analyst's eye? Am I to treat these photographs as if they were my patient, to develop a therapy for the pathology of images? Am I to psychoanalyze Jeff Jacobson based on these images, as if, like dreams, they were a subjective confession of his personal demons, a shadow projection on the world of his own pathologies and prejudices, a catharsis of his pain? Am I to explain his art by interpreting the revelations of personal history he makes in his introduction? Am I to be therapist and soften the sense of menace in these images? Are these the *appropriate* ways to help the viewer in witnessing *My Fellow Americans . . . ?* Are these my tasks?

If so, I refuse them. Not because I could not do so. I have learned well how to do these things. But ever since I saw Orozco's mural on the wall in Dartmouth Library—that image of the "gods of the modern world" in academic costume, with the background showing the world in flames and the foreground showing stillborn knowledge being delivered from a skeleton lying upon a bed of books — "dead things giving birth to dead things"—I have lost all heart to treat art with the tools of my trade. Better that such births be aborted early. I yearn for something *else,* some more fruitful conception.

To step outside the refuge of professional objectivity, to yield to this voice of yearning, exposes an embarrassing cacophony which simultaneously rouses shrouds of timidity and promptings to break out in loud shouting. It's the familiar state of the patient on the couch. Is this the key to discussing *My Fellow Americans . . .* ? To abandon explanation and interpretation. To couch myself, associating freely, letting go of ego. To open myself to these photographs as . . . *other.* To *tell* what happens there. If so, I find courage in Havelock Ellis' hint that this *is* the artist's method, whereby *reason and will are left aside; you trust to "an influx" and the faculties of mind are directed to ends they know not of.* Like a nervous, untrusting patient, there are initial resistances, rather like prejudices. These must be spoken first, clearing the way.

Art, probably earlier than any other human activity—excepting dreaming—reveals something of the nature of a new spirit of the time. Any period is characterized by a peculiar mixture of new spirits, aging spirits, ghostly spirits. One senses a new spirit loose in the world today. In the world of art it has been named "postmodern" because its intention and manifestation—most spectacularly the dissolution of *all* borders—contrasts so sharply with the highly bordered spirit of purity (no contamination by tradition, authority, or other influences) that was the virginal (sufficient unto itself) ideal of modernism. But clearly, all human activity, not just art, is subject now to the pervading wave of the postmodern impulse. Except in nemesis, this impulse is not the result of some conscious activity subject to willful decision, nor originated by powerful critics, or politicians, or the dynamics of money. Like all dramatic shifts in human consciousness, it arises from a deeper source.

What springs forth in images expressing something not yet known to the conscious mind, always carries something of the *future.* Perhaps the primary significance of a work of art—as well as of a dream—is what it engenders in response, what is enacted in return. This is why psychologizing art in terms of personal biography necessarily must fail. When psychology sees only through eyes of the past, and seeks out only the personal history, it impoverishes itself, does not open itself to the current of life emanating from the objective psyche. What is psychology's future?

Is it possible that *changes* in categories of psychological interpretation and therapy are being hinted at even now by what is showing itself in art? Can a work of art embody or engender a deeper revelation of the human psyche than psychology itself? Can psychology make itself vulnerable to the erotic spirit, in the sense imagined by H.G. Baynes: *The essential character of Eros is the divine (i.e., creative) shaft which leaps across the guarded frontier of the subject in order to reach the object. The creative shaft is the impregnating phallus, the impressive, fertilizing image, the creative word, the idea which gets home, the divine leap by which the individual subject is able to transcend his own subjectivity and take effective part in the work of creation. This is Eros, the god which bringeth twain together in the service of life.* Eros is a generative spirit crossing all borders, and when one welcomes this , opens oneself to it, as the artist does, one will take "effective part in the work of creation." Thus does eros gives birth to the future.

Interpretation so often yields nothing except the momentary relief of frustration—that frustration of "not knowing" what a work of art or a dream means. So often nothing is born of interpretation except a stultifying dependency upon it. The god of interpretation is not Eros.

We use this word 'interpretation' so quickly; we are carried along by an illusion of understanding. Paul Valéry said, ". . . we understand ourselves thanks only to the *speed of our passages past words.*" Valéry's idea applies as well to dreams, to images, to photographs. This suggests that slowing down, taking time, dwelling, with word or image provides the fertile ground upon which to be affected by the *other.* Silencing the ego's demands for interpretation, understanding, and meaning, coupled with slowing down, taking time, dwelling with: these are the crucial elements, all the introduction one needs, to prepare oneself for the eros of viewing when face to face with a word, an image, a dream, a photograph.

Photography began when the image of light could be held, held still, held indefinitely, remembered. *Photography is an art of exterior memory.* The camera as memory machine allows us to document and record events in the natural history of the world, in reality, the outer aspects of our experience. The camera remembers things we do not know because it can see things we cannot or did not see. But seen or not, sought or not, the camera remembers everything that touches that place of memory, that place we call *emulsion*—a technical photographic term, defined in the dictionary as "a light-sensitive coating, usually of silver halide salts in a thin gelatin layer." We clearly understand. But this understanding does not invite reverie, is not a stimulus to imagination, creates no desire to stop, to take time, to dwell with this word. Is there any eros in this word? How can we find the erotics of this word, its *intimacy*? One way is to unveil it, undress it, open the word's *memory* to view, find out what images lie hidden beneath the shell of this word. We do this by being curious about, caring for, attending to the word's origin, its ancestors, its story. To do this we must not just use the word. This habit leads to the abuse of the word. Instead, we must stop and listen for the word's history to echo to us. In this we become vulnerable to the word, led by the word. There is eros in that.

When we learn that the parent of emulsion is *melg-*, meaning "to milk," a reverie begins, resonating with sensibilities we did not have before. Emulsion is photography's milk-place, the source of nourishment, the mother-layer within the camera darkness. What is born there requiring milk? Does light suckle on silver there? This milky layer, this feminine film, is where light and silver dwell. They have intercourse there. The camera is not all male after all ("load," "aim," "shoot"). Does photography just pleasure itself there indiscriminately, a kind of prostitution where generation is not the aim? Or is something to be born there, nourished there? Or, more darkly, one cannot help noticing that "to milk" has come to mean "to exploit" and "to get money out of" and aren't these the characteristics of photography that so aroused Sontag's ire? When we photograph we milk reality for its truth. The photograph by its very nature is tied umbilically to *out there*—the real world of light—a cord that cannot be cut without losing itself and its privilege among the arts. Perhaps photography has the task of keeping "out there" before our eyes, to counteract in some crucial way our perdurable tendency to blind ourselves to what needs to be seen. Exploitation is not the only way to imagine what takes place there. Spending time with the words of photography, seeking out their etymology ("truth speaking"), letting the images released penetrate and evoke, is one way to respond to the impoverished language of photography.

Psychoanalysis, like photography, also began with memory, in the recovery of memories forgotten through the agencies of repression. *Psychology is an art of internal memory.* Psychology too needed to "fix" the image, to keep it in mind, to keep it in the emulsion of awareness. Analysts seized upon the dream, if it could be remembered, as the royal road to the unconscious, in much the same way as photographers seized upon the camera as the "royal road to reality." The dream, embodying an interior world, presents itself to the conscious mind in much the same way a photograph presents an embodied external world. There is a curious symmetry between dream and photographs, but these similarities have yet to be essayed fully. Like the photograph, the dream is a kind of frozen moment, and almost always is treated as if it is to be understood only by reference to the past.

Barthes says that *whether or not the subject is already dead, every photograph is this catastrophe.* There is no doubt that death lurks in every photograph, and it is this flight from death, so prominent in our time, that causes our fascination with and preference for images that *move.* In contrast, the *stillness* of the photographic image, its *silence,* its *suspension,* all contribute to an awareness of finality. We must, however, consider this: The moment frozen and preserved in the photographic image points as well to the *future.* The moment captured on film was, always is, and ever will be *mother* to what followed. More than this: Every photograph is a progenitor, always birthing a future. Its eros lies there. In what comes next. But where is this *next*?

It has been argued that photographs do not tell a story, do not narrate. Because of this, *next* is frequently the next image, the next photographs, the flight from image to image. It is unimportant that photographs fail to narrate. They do not. But there is a more critical *next* that is frequently unattended. It is the spontaneous manifestations of the psyche. The psyche does respond to the image narratively, particularly if this spontaneity is not blocked or constrained or bordered by the ego's too ready need for interpretation. Even so, ego understanding is only one narrative among many, and more inclined toward repetition and habit than is the *spontaneous* response of the psyche to the *shock* of a photograph. It may be important that the photograph catch hold of a truth, or represent a truth. But true as well, and perhaps more interesting, is the question of what lies in the narrative response of the spontaneous psyche.

Go back and view the photographs in *My Fellow Americans . . . ,* forget about meaning, forget about Jacobson's intentions, forget about art. Let the image seep into you. Look at the first picture. Look for an hour. Resist turning the page. Resist movement. Stay there. Look deeply. Let the image in. All of it. See what rises up in you. What does the image want you to do? Will you do it? What fantasies come? Is this a mirror? Don't just preen or shiver with recognition: step *through* it, like Alice. Is this a window? Climb in, or climb out. Keep going. Fantasies are brewing; memories are coming. The image is alive in you now, generating, weaving stories. Tell the story out loud. Never mind if no one's there. Watch what you dream tonight.

To set aside the demand for interpretation, to slow down, to take time to dwell with the image—in photograph, in dream—to suffer the hunger for instant resolution to the problem of meaning, to quiet the noisy ego, to open oneself to the spontaneity of the psyche, to let eros as *other* in. These are some of the sensibilities that seem to me essential for the ritual of viewing a dream or a photograph.

I find Barthes' distinction between *studium*—as the result of the photographer's conscious intention—and *punctum*—as that element in the photograph which triggers an entailing narrative that catches him up in *its* spin, *its* weaving, to be very helpful. This is not something that results from interpretation of the photograph; it results from some element in the photograph breaking through the conscious borders and uniting with something in the realm beyond one's consciousness. This is eros, and, as Baynes said, it leads to an effective participation in the work of creation. A story is born. Stories must be told. So part of the work of creation, part of the work that helps to bring the future in, is to tell the stories induced in us. It is this telling of stories engendered by art and dream that becomes the erotic basis for enactment in the world, the continuing work for creation.

The silent solitude of the still image sets loose a roaring cascade! The photograph is *psychoactive.* I forget to inquire after its meaning. I fail to notice the caption. I seem not to care where this piece of reality took place, for now it's taking place in me. Some critic, or my analyst, shouts, "Narcissism! Why muck about in your own images? What has that to do with the photographer's intentions, what he's created, the meaning of his art?" For a moment, I'm caught by this, try to hold back the rush of images and feelings, make a dike; but hands are useless against a wave. There goes an image of that book

I'll write on the symmetry of the photograph and dream (will I do it?) and in the middle of my resolve lands that heron again, wings wide, looking at me intently. Is he (or is he she?) wondering if I get the hint? I look at Jeff's photograph of the old couple holding a photograph; I'll be in that scene, holding photographs, too, not too long from now. That doesn't disturb me; I look forward to then. What disturbs me is that *rope*, that's what punctures me. My eyes are fascinated by that rope hanging down from the tree ("remnant of a hanging rope," some voices chorus), like the hearing aid dangling from the old man's ear. Is the tree hard of hearing? Is it my own failure to hear, projected there on that rope? Will I be hung there on a tree hard of hearing? Or is that the first line of a poem I'll never write, like lots of poems never written, just like Jack Kerouac's imagined poet writing from the pictures of Robert Frank's *The Americans*, the poet still trapped there in Jack's imagination, more tightly imprisoned than before. Wait! There's a door, it's opening, poets are streaming out, like Michelangelo's strugglers coming out of stone. Stop! This is crazy. Quick, look at another picture.

In my reverie, *My Fellow Americans . . .* becomes a dream, the impossible dream, an open letter to us from a *truth-telling* president. A letter without words, because words have become as empty and untrue as our cherished forms and rituals. Instead, he opens the masks that cover our last sanctuary—everyday life—invites us to peer in, lets the high horror see us directly, lets us stare back though we have become transfixed, paralyzed, not knowing what to do. Everyone grasps for the black and white of certainty, but this reach is obliterated continually by a carnival of color, where nothing can be seen as it was meant to be seen, seen instead, now, how it *must* be seen: the smiling mask unveiled revealing what no one dare say. I'm witness to a president filled with daring showing his people the true sickness of soul pervading the land, showing his people in whose servitude they are employed, showing his people that he and they still lust after *Moby Dick*, while the soulfood for a whole nation has become but a single dead pigeon. I'm amazed to hear our president say that as a people we are shrinking, as the gods we pursue, dressed brightly as colored tins, grow larger and larger. He asks us to question their godly status. Amazing! Our president confesses that his superman which we believed in is mask only, tomorrow it comes off; no more poses, no more pretend. But tonight he is preoccupied, looking at her . . . . I see him show the curtain's come down, the play's over, the bench sags. He cannot promise if America will hold. In my vision I see millions of us with hands to our ears, hands to our eyes, hands to our mouths. One by one this changes. Each now looks with eyes open. We are looking together at *My Fellow Americans . . .* , watching there all the hands, all the eyes. Looking at the mouths of babes. I'm not alone. Others see the menace, too.

"Is there any hope?" we plead. The dream president shows us that salvation lies with the children yet pictures us devouring our children, starving them, sacrificing them to feed the plastic of the cabbage patch. More menace in that. Still, that last image . . . that child . . . the grandfather . . . the love there . . . something now about another grandpa. . . yes—or maybe I'll go Southwest, follow the trail of my great, great grandfather, maybe.

Wake up America. Take a look. Jeff Jacobson has taken our picture when we weren't looking. In a time when "know thyself" has been replaced by "be known by others," we search frantically for our self, for our soul in the eyes of others. Well, here we are, revealed. We're running on empty. Our common ruin.

At first I thought all the red so striking in these photographs might be the blood that photography extracts from reality—fifty million photographs a day—making the image more alive than reality itself. But that's not it. Then I thought it might be the rocket's red glare of our national anthem of self-destruction. But that's not it, either. Then, I dreamed *My Fellow Americans . . .* was a "prayer book." The dream wants us to see all this red as the rubricating consecration of a new common missal—a prayer book for our time. In time?

Russell Lockhart

Acknowledgments

I am blessed with many wonderful friends and family. Their love and laughter helped me to make the pictures in this book. The photographs in *My Fellow Americans . . .* were made over a long period of my life, more than thirteen years. Consequently, many people had a hand in helping me with my work, in different ways, at different times. One of the pleasures of publishing this book is remembering those people and being able to publicly acknowledge them. Specifically, I want to thank Nubar Alexanian, Fina Bathrick, Olin Dodson, Harold Eisenman, Lorraine Ferguson, Bill Fibben, Alice Rose George, Donald Gropman, Charlie Harbutt, Annette and Harold Jacobson, Alain Jullien, Gus Kaufman, Meryl Levin, Joan Liftin, Russ Lockhart, Kenny Mirvis, Susan O'Connor, Sylvia Plachy, Lena Ross, Lauren Shaw, Mary Shea, Alex Webb, and Adam D. Weinberg.

Abigail Heyman and Ethan Hoffman, my publishers and my friends, fought valiantly for this book. *My Fellow Americans . . .* is stronger because Abby and Ethan gave so much of themselves to it.

We lost Ethan awhile back—he died in a freak accident while photographing. He was my publisher at the Picture Project, my partner at Archive, and always my friend. I miss him every day.

J.J.